55 Techniques on

How to Blow Him

Away

With hot Blow Jobs

Practical Guild to Mind Blowing Oral sex
Techniques

That will Drive Him Crazy.

Frank White

TABLE OF CONTENT

INTRODUCTION

You might be reading this to get ready for his birthday, your anniversary, for a first meeting, or just out of general interest (and if this is the case, bless your heart). Whatever your motivation, this book covers all you may need to know about giving your partner the best blowjob he's ever had.

Looking for guidance or more information on fellatio? We are willing to assist with any inquiry, no matter how dumb. What precisely is fellatio then? How can you perform fellatio more effectively, and where did it emerge from? It's simpler than you think to provide a blowjob of the highest calibre that will change lives, open hearts, and awaken neighbours.

Oral sex may seem routine and a natural aspect of foreplay to most people, but for individuals who have never given a blow job before, it may be terrifying and intimidating. If you fit into the latter group, we bet you have many queries for him regarding oral.

90% of men think it's fantastic when women give them a blowout; nevertheless, women must vary it up and avoid being too organized, as there's a significant chance they'll grow weary of it. There is a wide variety of blowjob positions, ranging from the most traditional, with a calm man resting on his back, to the fastidious one, when a denuded female partner at the highest level completely overwhelms all of her male partner's senses. Considering that a blowjob position mostly depends on your partner's preferences, consider all his thoughts and needs. The blowjob involves using the hands, mouth, fingers, expert tongue, and even the breast: caress the penis sensually, be rude, and the outcome will not take long. Many women find blowjobs intolerable, but remember that when you use one, you have complete control over the male and can do whatever you want with him.

Anyone's fellatio game can be improved from mediocre to expert with a few basic techniques in their back pocket.To that end, before we even discuss anatomy, technique, or logistics, let's discuss the code that will enable the game's top levels. Anyone can be "good" if they have the treasure map and all the necessary components. However, one cornerstone is frequently missed that will make your oral presentation epic.

Chapter 1

What is fellatio

The phrase fellatio is the medical name for blow jobs or oral for him, as we've already hinted at. However, it's crucial to remember that fellatio does not imply cunnilingus and instead refers to him as oral (oral sex for her). Using your mouth to stimulate a man's penis is known as fellatio, to put it simply.

Where did fellatio originate?

Quite a challenge, this. Despite anecdotal evidence of fellatio being a common sexual practice throughout history, it is difficult to pinpoint the act's specific origins. Even worse, fellatio might have always been a component of sex when done in private.

There is no doubt, however, that oral for him appears to be a practice that is commonplace globally and that the act of fellatio is not isolated to one or a few tribes or civilizations. Essentially, if you're thinking about trying fellatio for the first time, you may relax knowing that you are neither the first nor the last person to do so.

How to perform fellatio

Feeling a little lost when it comes to where to begin while learning fellatio? Let's start with the foundations. Ensure that you are 100 per cent comfortable with the idea of trying oral sex with your spouse before making the decision. Although it's okay to be anxious, you shouldn't give a fellatio if you're not comfortable with the idea.

Security is a crucial factor that fellatio must also take into account. STIs are still a severe worry even though you won't become pregnant due to giving your partner fellatio. Make sure both of you have undergone testing and have clean health certificates. Never hesitate to use a condom if you're unsure.

Now that everything has been verified as safe and you are ready to try giving your lover oral, all that is left to do is perform the act. That might be where your anxiety lies if you are a complete fellatio novice. Do not be alarmed; we have your back. For peace of mind and thorough preparation, look out for our 5-step tutorial on how to give fellatio right now.

How to perform deepthroat fellatio

This section probably isn't for you if you've never spoken to him orally before. The place is where you should be if, on the other hand, you believe you have mastered the fundamentals and want to improve your fellatio skills. The sensual world of deepthroat fellatio will now be examined.

So, when we use the term "deepthroat," what precisely do we mean? The idea is straightforward; the challenge is putting it into practice. When performing fellatio, "deepthroat" refers to taking your partner's penis into your mouth while allowing your throat to accept the business end.

Feeling challenging? It can be, which is why. You won't be able to pick it up quickly, and it will probably take a lot of practice until you master it. Because of this, we do not advise you to try it out for yourself. The most excellent way to improve the skill is to practice it regularly with a partner.

How to make fellatio more enjoyable

Let's be honest: after finishing your first session of sucking, you might have realized that it's not for you. That's right, and it truly doesn't matter. We can't stress this enough. There are plenty of other things you may do in the bedroom to make your lover happy if

giving fellatio is not something you want to
do again.

Chapter 2

How To Get Started

What to do

A little old-fashioned making out is the best way to make a move.

Get them ready by kissing and stroking some of their other erogenous areas, such as their neck and ears.

Take a seat in that position.

There is no need to try complex sex positions as long as you both feel at ease enough to enjoy it. They had the option of standing, sitting, or lying flat on their back as their lips lingered over them while you knelt in front of them.Suppose you can make eye contact while in this position, bonus points. Eye contact increases intimacy, conveys confidence, is sexy, and is super hot.

If you'd like, take off your clothes.Clothing is optional unless you're in a location where you can't go naked. Your comfort level will ultimately determine what you do.It can be done without removing the rest of their clothing by pulling his underwear down to expose their entire anatomy.

Consider going all out if the sensation of skin on skin makes you both feel heated.

Steps for moving your tongue

I mean, anything goes. When climbing up and down the shaft, use your whole tongue.You can focus on the more delicate, smaller portions of your body using the tip of your tongue. The frenulum can be flicked with the information; then, you can gently place them in your mouth after softly swirling them around the head.

What to do with a full mouth?

Concentrate on chewing them at a pace that says "mmm, mmm good" rather than "just come and let's get this over with already."
Increase your pace gradually while starting slowly and lightly. Keep going, even if it seems like the action is about to reach a climax.

How do you know? Their physical expression!

Be aware of what your hips are doing as you descend because they don't lie. There are several indications that they are enjoying it and nearing the climax, including thrusting, maintaining a stable head position, or shivering.

Keeping your teeth out of the way

Your teeth should not be an issue here unless you're trying to bite down. But we recognize some people worry about unintentional dental contact (yes, brace-wearing folks!).Allowing your tongue and lips to touch is all that is necessary. Just like that, your teeth will vanish and merge into the scenery.

How to make your voice next-level hot in the workplace

Go ahead and shout! Although talking with your mouth full may be impolite, the sounds you make as you do so let them know you are savouring every last inch of them, which is a significant turn-on.

Nom, nom, noms are unnecessary because there isn't even a lick of gelato. You enjoy it if you moan, breathe heavily, or even suck. They'll also find the vibration from your mouth very pleasant.

Using your hands correctly.

Get emotional when you're speaking. By controlling the depth with your hand, you may also lavish extra attention on different areas of your body.

Stroke the shaft with your hand, and when you get to the head, let your thumb brush the frenulum. While licking and sucking, you can carry on doing this.Put your ability to multitask by massaging your balls with your other hand.

Incorporating penetration

Do it when someone permits you to stick your finger in their butt. Use a lot of lubrication, that's all.Use the pads of your index and middle fingers to gently press on their perineum before slipping an incredibly lubricated finger inside their anus.If you and your partner are OK with it, take rimming a step further by sticking the tip of your tongue into their anus and poking it in and out.

How to include sex toys

It is best to gradually and liberally add toys to the mix with lubrication.

For instance, you can tease the opening by inserting a butt plug slowly after using the tip. Keep the butt plug in a while, licking and massaging it for twice the pleasure—possibly even an anal orgasm.

How to keep moving forward or when to halt

You don't need to stop unless they've instructed you to or your jaw is excruciatingly sore and cramping. You decide entirely. If you're stuck for ideas, check out these.You should proceed if they want you to.Stick with what you're doing since it's likely to be effective if you're willing to keep it.With a few well-placed groans and eye contact, you may increase your momentum and energy and move them along more quickly.

If he is Ready to Cum

Even if you let them complete in your mouth, you won't feel pressure to swallow.As you continue sucking, allow the semen to enter your slightly opened lips. Take a gulp now if you're going to. Otherwise, you can quietly spit it out into a nearby cup or piece of cloth, which is much hotter than it sounds, or let it drip down your chin.

If you don't like tapioca's texture, switch to giving them a hand immediately before the climax if you prefer that. Letting them finish on your chin, chest, or another part of your body is OK.

Stop whenever you want

And remember that just because the BJ component of the program is completed doesn't mean that sexy time has to end if you're not ready for it.

Start kissing your way back up their body after interpreting it as foreplay. You can then proceed in any direction. It is advised to climb on them, roll over, or guide them down so they can verbally retort.

Things to remember

1:Each body is unique. Forget what you've seen in porn, where the penis usually is large, smooth as eggplant, and complimented for taste "oh so nice" while an equally beautiful tongue handles it.

2:Everybody has a unique sense of taste and scent.

Your distinct smell can be impacted by various factors, including what you eat and the soap you use. Furthermore, it is impossible to anticipate removing a penis from the constrictive space of pants without leaving some sweat or stink.

3:Usually, all that's needed to keep things clean down there is a quick shower. What slight smell remains is entirely acceptable and natural.

The taste of someone's bodily fluids can vary depending on various conditions, just like their natural odour. Drinking more water, consuming less red meat, and reducing smoking are all things that someone with a weird taste can do to help freshen it up.

4:Numerous hues, patterns, and sizes can be seen in pubic hair and penises.
5:When it comes to physical traits, penises are incredibly diverse.

There are still risks associated with oral sex.

There are STIs that spread through the mouth. Any touch with bodily fluids or skin-to-skin contact might spread STIs.Do not be deceived by packaging that appears to be healthy. The symptoms of STIs vary. Try using flavoured condoms to lessen your risk and treat yourself to something tasty.

Inquiries that are frequently asked.

We'll start with the most important ones since I'm sure you have some questions now.

If the foreskin is present, what should you do?

The foreskin doesn't require you to make any changes to your gameplay. Letting the foreskin move with your hand is best if you start with your hands.Pull the foreskin gently to expose the head when ready to continue.

How might gagging be prevented?

Although some might (literally) beg to differ, gabbing does not constitute a decent blow job. You can prevent gag reflexes by blocking your throat with the tip of your tongue.

Has your throat become deep?

Only if you choose to, even without delving deeply, can you still provide a mind-blowing beej. Instead, position it such that it is facing your mouth's roof. They likely won't understand the difference unless your companion is an oral surgeon.

How do you tell whether everything is alright?

There's nothing you can do to mess this up than taking a mouthful. Be on the lookout for nonverbal cues to enjoyment, such as heavier, faster breathing or thrusting.

Don't be shy about asking if radio silence feels good if it's making you nervous. The fact that you sincerely desire to win their favour will undoubtedly attract them.

If your mouth becomes fatigued, what should you do?

Use your hands. It's equally as fun to switch between the hand and mouth!

If you swallow, does it matter?Your degree of comfort is what ultimately matters. You and your partner should first discuss it.

Having someone finish on your closed lips or chin can be just as sexy if swallowing semen isn't your thing. Some individuals adore the image of completing in someone's mouth.

How To Receive A Blowjob

Even though the person getting a BJ typically doesn't have to put in as much effort as the person delivering it, there are a few things you can and should do to ensure your partner is comfortable.

1:Bring a tidy dick with you.It may seem obvious, but it's crucial to clean before oral sex.

2:A dirty pole doesn't need a tongue bath.
Being considerate of your partner is a fantastic notion, even if everyone has a distinctive aroma, and it is nothing to be ashamed of.
Therefore, take a shower if you've just returned from a 30-mile bike ride or an exercise session at the gym.Use regular soap and water; there is no need to scrub yourself or take any particular precautions. It only needs that.

3:Be mindful of your comfort.

You can't expect your partner to have fun if they suffer from rug burns on their knees while sucking you off, so make sure you and they are both comfortable.Your partner's neck will appreciate it if you occasionally switch positions if you're engaged in a prolonged physical altercation.

In an identical vein, wait until you've been given the go-ahead before grabbing your partner's head and sticking your cock into their gaping mouth!Although it may be a familiar image in some pornography, that is not how life is.You risk inflicting an equally swift dick injury if you try that rapid action on an unprepared partner.

4:Be considerate and provide helpful criticism.When getting a blowjob, don't be afraid to say what you enjoy and don't like.Although keeping things a little mysterious might be enjoyable, you shouldn't leave your spouse in the dark.

The things your partner likes and dislikes should also be known to you, as this is very crucial. Some individuals prefer raw and sloppy, while others are more subdued and orderly.Contrary to popular belief, giving a BJ doesn't have to be a dull or unpleasant experience for the giver.

Are flavoured lubricants popular with your partner? How about flavour-infused condoms? Is it essential to your partner that you share your feelings with them?Keep in mind that you should be participating in the enjoyment in either case!

What Are the Dangers of Fellatio?

Fellatio is not entirely risk-free, even if it is less dangerous than analingus or vaginal intercourse.Unless you are aware of your status and that of your partner and are convinced that you don't require protection, it is commonly recommended to use a condom. You can still contract many STDs during oral intercourse, including HPV.

Make sure the lubricant you're using is designed to be eaten if you're using one to make oral sex more enjoyable for everyone.It's okay to eat edible lubricants, which are often water-based.

Choking on lubrication during oral sex can be more than just a buzzkill; it can be rather deadly. Some lubricants, such as those that are oil-based, are not safe to swallow.Additionally, if you're wearing a condom, check to make sure your lube won't degrade it.Maintaining a water-based lubricant intended to be eaten is your best bet.

Chapter 3

The Best 20 Blowjob Positions To Experiment With

A variety of alternatives are available for the satisfaction of the provider and receiver while fellating is in full flow. I've compiled a list of my top picks below to simplify things, emphasising the male viewpoint.

1: The Pivot

The lady positions herself 90 degrees apart from the male on his back, either propped up on her knees or completely lying down, perpendicular to him.For various reasons, this is an absurdly appealing position for him.

He may insert a finger inside you from here, or he can rub, squeeze, and caress his favourite places on your body. While you can create sporadic eye contact, he can view almost all of your facial features and curves.

He can completely unwind and experience every little wave of pleasure that flows through him. You can also relaxly rub his anus or perineum while massaging his thighs.

2:King's Chair

This is one of the best blowjob positions because it accentuates the power dynamic, which is a big part of why some men find getting a blowjob so satisfying.The male is sitting upright in the chair, and the lady kneels between his legs, where she has full access to his thighs, perineum, and anus.This is a fantastic method if you want to make him feel respected and served. This pose is INCREDIBLY sexy when you use that note of making a little eye contact.Although he is the intended recipient of the entire event, as I previously stated, stoking your enjoyment is what will ultimately fuel his. This is a fantastic moment to play with yourself or add a vibrator to the mix while enjoying his company.

3. Continual Support

This blowjob is one of the best. The power dynamic is well-expressed, much like in the previous position. When a woman kneels in front of him, the male stands completely upright.The benefits and downsides of standing up are both there. In addition, he can get a little more involved by thrusting into your mouth or throat. On the good side, it feels hot for both of you. Also, from there, he can ejaculate upon you from a particularly scorching vantage point.

The fact that he must contract his leg and glute muscles prevents him from relaxing entirely in that position. The total effect and intensity of his orgasm, if any, are ultimately diminished.

4:Doggy Fashion

The male is on his knees, and the woman is in front of him on all fours, just like the standard doggie penetration technique. She was using her mouth rather than her vagina, facing the other way.

This has similar advantages to the previous position in that the man can thrust slightly if he chooses and enjoy the scorching experience of being serviced. In this posture, he will have much more sensation and be able to have a bigger orgasm because he is using less effort to support himself.

Because of the angle and necessity to use at least a hand or elbow to support yourself, the only negatives are that you can only make limited eye contact and operate with your hands and mouth with intensity.

5:The Lie Back

The woman is lying on her back with her head barely protruding over the edge of the bed in this position. Invading her throat, the man either stands or kneels near the border. In this situation, most of the power is mainly in the male's hands, but the female can add additional stimulation with her hands.

He gets to be in charge while enjoying a sensual and flattering view of your body, which makes this a beautiful scenario. From this position, he can also massage your breasts or energise you.

Because this posture is suitable for deep throating, it's essential to take care if your gag reflex is particularly sensitive (I'll discuss how you might train to change that a little later in this article). But if you stay in touch, you can thoroughly enjoy this while he either lasts inside your mouth or gradually tests the waters while advancing deeper. A pinch of his thigh could serve as your "that's too much" signal.

6:Snake charmer

Description:

By playing an instrument and moving it around, snake charmers in India may hypnotize snakes. Use a fantastic blowjob to mesmerize your partner and drive him crazy. Straight-legged and holding out his arms, the man is perched on the edge of the chair. On the borders of the furniture, his palms are resting. Leaning back, his body. A lady approaches a man's penis while crouching between his legs, bending her upper body to get closer. With her tongue and hands, she alternately caresses the penis.

7:A tea bag

Description:

Unexpectedly, a man has erogenous areas other than his penis. Even if he'd want to believe that his scrotum is his largest sex organ. The woman is lying on her back with her head dangling off the side of the bed. Her feet are placed on the ground while she flexes her legs. The male partner precisely positions his face between his legs while he stands with his back to the bed. The man supports the mistress's nape as she places her palms on his hips, allowing her to feel at ease in such a novel posture.

8:Whisper

Description:

The male partner will be enamoured with your efforts if you delicately and tenderly caress his penis with your mouth, especially in this posture where he is just lying down and enjoying. With his arms stretched out along his torso and his legs straight and spaced apart, the man lies on his back on the pillow in a roughly equivalent position to half-sitting. The female partner is lying on his stomach with her face in front of his penis, her hands helping to caress his penis, and her legs positioned next to one another with her knees bent. He has the option of moving his female partner's head, grabbing her by the hair, or simply admiring the lovely image.

9:Loop

Description:

The blowjob is perhaps the hardest in this posture. Due to the great vision and the woman only touching his penis with her lips, it is intended to give men heaven-like pleasure. His straight legs are splayed widely apart as he lays on his back. Between his thighs, facing his penis and testicles, the female partner assumes a bridge pose à la yoga. Her palms are concealed beneath his buttocks as she places her hands on the lover's loin on either side. A man can play with a woman's breasts and nipples while performing a blowjob.

10:Niagara Falls

Description:

The most famous falls in the world are undoubtedly Niagara Falls. Yet, due to the extreme acrobatics and flexibility needed, the Niagara falls sex position is hardly ever seen. However, it is foreign, hot, and enjoyable. The man is standing with his feet shoulder-width apart and is slightly slanting to one side. He is somewhat bent over on one knee. As she approaches the man's penis, the woman gracefully arches while standing with her back to him. As she provides oral gratification to her male companion, she grabs her lover by the hip to balance and steady her body. Besides enjoying the stunning view, the man also supports her by placing his hand beneath her back.

11:Moan

Description:

Scream and moan without restraint. Talking about sex in a sexually explicit manner enables partners to communicate. Try the Moan fellatio to knock your man's socks off in the bedroom if you're up for some experimentation! To balance his body, the male partner lies on the fitness ball on his back, bringing his hands back to rest, palms down on the floor on the other side of the ball. He slightly crooks his knees and spreads his legs extremely wide. Leaning forward with her upper body, the lady kneels down between his legs and starts caressing his penis with her tongue, fingers, or any other way that comes to her filthy mind.

12:blowjob insanity

Description:

Most men enjoy blowjobs because they allow them to feel in charge briefly and enjoy seeing women submit. If you have the flexibility to win your man's heart, attempt this stunning posture. In a bridge stance a la yoga, the female partner places herself. In front of the woman, he kneels. The body posture of the male partner is maintained. He slightly repositions his arms. She gives him a deep throat blowjob while encircling her partner's penis in her mouth. He can occasionally assist her with his hands, but he must do it properly, or she may lose her ability to balance her body.

13:Sexual Slave

Description:

If you want to demonstrate your loyalty and commitment to your one and only partner and that you are at ease around him as you are around yourself take on his most sultry oral cravings and demonstrate what a free woman is capable of. On his back, the man raises his upper torso with his elbows while straightening his knees. Standing between his legs while prostrated, the female partner gives her male spouse oral gratification. You may be sure that your male partner will adore this position because most guys enjoy watching women perform blowjobs.

14:Compliment

Description:

Give her praise as she enjoys all of your favourite parts! Both she and he find this posture to be quite comfortable and enjoyable. With his legs widely apart, the man kneels on the edge of the bed. A tight embrace between the woman's legs and the furniture's foot characterizes her sitting position. She leans her upper body forward as she places her palms on her partner's buttocks. Each guy is affected differently by pressure, pace, and rhythm, so he grabs her face in his hands and advises a steady beat.

15:Soldier

Description:

You are the most acceptable person to assist your exhausted man in relaxing and ensure that the process is quick and painless. The male-only needs to lay on his back in a posture that is cosy for him. The woman lies close by and rests her head at the base of his belly while also blowing kisses on his penis with one hand. Without sure this occurrence will discourage your male companion, but the reality is that he will appreciate your initiative. Do not worry if you are new to oral sex; the important thing is to be gentle and not be scared to try new things.

15:Marsh-mallow

Description:

Such a posture will assist you in your quest if your male spouse is exhausted from work and you want to reward him for a hard day's labour, or you have decided to produce something lovely for him. The male partner lies on his back with his legs spread apart and his hands placed along the body with the palms up. The woman bends forward while sitting between the male partner's legs on her feet and embracing his hips with her hands. For a man, this is a wonderfully relaxed posture for oral gratification. It may be an excellent choice for both foreplay and the complete satisfaction of the male partner.

16:Croissant

Description:

The male has the option to take the lead during the procedure, which will enthral him more and more. In this posture, the lady can thoroughly swallow the man's penis. The partner lies on his back with his legs spread wide and slightly bent at the knees. The woman leans forward with her body so that her head is between his legs as she stands in front of him with her legs open on his knees. He places his hands on her head and regulates the intensity and frequency of movement. If the male partner desires it, his mistress's hands and mouth can caress his penis.

17:Symphony

Description:

Many men adore oral sex and will try to convince a woman to engage in this type of closeness. Engaging in this type of sexual activity should not be commonplace; this fact needs to be acknowledged. The man is on his back with his head propped up on a pillow. He raises his straight legs and drives his hips apart from the inside. The woman truly makes mouth movements while sitting in front of the male partner on her feet, bends forward, places her hands on his buttocks, and stimulates his penis with her hands.

18:Discharge

Description:

When a man feels weak, he may sometimes refuse sex or have a weak erection. Use this position to facilitate sexual activity with your male partner. The man is on his back with his legs at shoulder width. The female partner crouches down between his knees and crosses her legs over his to place his hands on her just above her feet. One hand is placed on the partner's stomach, and the other is used to activate his penis. She has her entire body tilted forward to perform oral sex, massaging her man's mouth and arousing him.

19:Blade

Description:

Oral sex should also be varied so that the partners do not regard it as a routine, continually search for new approaches, and acquire top-notch impressions. The man lies on his side with his legs spread apart and bent at the knees, his feet positioned crosswise, and his upper torso raised on one elbow. The woman rests on her side with her hand resting on her partner's thigh while her legs are straight and squeezed together to form a circle around the man's legs. The man places his other hand on his female partner's hand on his thigh so that he can stroke it and, of course, feel the excitement.

20:Guillotine

Description:

This guillotine is a blowjob sex position intended to drive the man insane rather than being used for beheading executions. Learn how to deliver your man the most OK blow job he's ever experienced. The woman is lying on her back. The female partner's head is positioned between the legs of the male partner seated on top of her. The man only partially sits on the woman; he places the most pressure on his knees, which are positioned behind the female partner's shoulders. She extends her lower body upward, spreads her legs wide, and places them on her partner's shoulders. He pulls his hands back and grabs her buttocks to support the woman in this unusual position. He is her only boss, period. The male partner's body remains straight. With her lips, mouth, and tongue, the woman arouses her lover's penis.

Blowjob Foundational Advice

Take the remaining third into your mouth, and with a well-lubricated hand, stroke the lower two-thirds of his shaft up and down (where most of his sensation is.) To prevent teeth contact, maintain a light "O" shape with your lips (avoid doing this at all costs!).

Once in a while, you might remove him from your mouth and lick his frenulum, which is his most delicate area, or keep your tongue there while you continue to stroke him. Attempt flicking, circling, or side-to-side tongue movement while performing this.

Recall his remaining genitalia as well.

The base of the shaft of the scrotum, which typically feels fantastic as well, can be licked while you continue to stroke. You might delicately put one or both testicles in your mouth and gently rub it with your tongue (but check with your man whether he likes this because some men are too sensitive for this, which can hurt them).

You can raise your stroking hand to stroke the glans and frenulum for maximum stimulation while leaving the tip of his penis free.

You can play with his testicles and scrotum while using the significant motions of the fundamental techniques by lightly undulating your hand and applying a delicate tug with your free hand. It is comparable to an excellent song with a lot more bass. It completes the overall impression and gives the emotion a powerful undertone.

Using this moment, I'd like to point out that being within your mouth isn't the BEST thing to do and is simply a tiny component of a blowjob. While the word "blowjob" implies much, the actual purpose is to use your hands and mouth to provide tremendous genital pleasure. The most intense sensation will typically come from your licks on these other areas, such as the scrotum or frenulum while being inside your mouth combined with stroking is a surefire way to finish him off.

Variation.

Just enough to mix things up is necessary. The entire song shouldn't be played on a single note, but you shouldn't move too quickly as you stick to one thing at a certain intensity, pleasure increases. Allow yourself to examine him freely, but linger in each location to gauge his reaction. You could repeat the action for 30 to 60 seconds at a time.

Chapter 4

55 Intense Blow Job Techniques That Will Make Him Scream With Pleasure!

If you want to make your boyfriend utterly dependent on you—or any man, for that matter—you must be familiar with the best blow job techniques to induce orgasmic joy.

To teach you 55 of my most powerful blow job techniques, this chapter of the Blow Job Guide is all about that.

Let's now learn how to perform a blow job such that your man's toes curl up in pleasure and his eyes roll into the back of his head.

- **To be licked repeatedly.**

One effective way to start a blow job is by licking the target's penis. It acts as a form of oral sex foreplay that increases sexual tension and makes him beg for you to take him in your mouth—precisely what you want.

It's a breeze to lick his cock. The simplest method is to lick his penis while holding it in your hands. Licking him from base to tip turns out to be an effective method. You can utilize a variety of various licking methods during your blow job, so don't stop here:

- **Focus on the Tip:** According to one study, the underside of your guy's glans which is located on the top section of his penis, or the glans, is the part of his penis that is most sensitive. However, the sensitivity will be slightly reduced if your man has been circumcised. The frenulum is also quite sensitive and is located on the bottom side where the head attaches to the shaft. However, some research indicates that the entire glans is exposed, with no one area being more sensitive than the others [3].

- Use as little pressure as you can while concentrating on licking his glans, which is the tip of his penis. According to many guys, this is the ultimate favourite blow job technique. You might even try doing this during the entire blowout until he arrives. More about the tip of his penis being orally gratified.

- My exclusive and discreet newsletter has the orgasms you need to give your partner the back-arching, toe-curling, screaming orgasms that will keep him addicted to you sexually. Along with how to avoid them, you'll discover the five risky & "stupid" sex errors that turn him off. Get it right here.

- **The Topside of Your Tongue**: Because of the rough surface that your taste buds produce, the topside of your tongue stimulates you a little more than the underneath.

- **Recall his balls;** they are essential. For some guys, their balls are even more sensitive than their penis. The most straightforward approach to stimulate his balls for optimum enjoyment is to lick them, but I also detail numerous other methods in this section.

- In addition to his penis and balls, Anilingus has two fantastic spots where you may significantly increase his enjoyment and make him think of you as a queen of oral sex, even if they are not exactly a part of a conventional BJ.

- Many nerve endings can be found in his anus and perineum, often known as the perineal raphe or "taint," a rough region of skin directly behind his balls. You can stimulate his penis through his perineum because the root of it is hidden behind this skin, behind the perineum [4, 5]. Some males love nothing more than to have these two places licked and stimulated, while others don't care for it at all. Your man will determine what you prefer; it's a personal choice.

- It's an excellent method to stimulate them to tongue these areas up and down or in a circular motion. To create a new but equally wonderful sensation, press your tongue inward into his anus. The term "anilingus" refers to this method.

- **Taint-To-Tip**: Licking your man slowly from his perineum up to the tip of his penis is a terrific method if he has sensitive perineum (taint) or balls. It works best if you do this in a single, steady, continuous lick.

Using your hand or just a finger to press his penis on his belly can make it simpler for you to perform the act.

When licking his dick during a blow job, it's imperative to remember the following:

- The weather is better.

- The best blow jobs are wet; any male will agree with you. However, it's not always easy to manufacture large amounts of saliva on demand.
- The following are two tips for increasing salivation:
- Shortly before descending upon him, chew gum.
- Before you start blowing him, eat some juicy fruit (like a strawberry, pineapple, or peach).
- These two techniques don't work every time, of course.
- Use edible lube to create incredibly wet blow jobs; it's more straightforward and dependable. Just keep some accessible in your purse or a drawer beside your bed.

As a result, you will also be prepared should you require lubricant during sex.

- Solution for Deep Throating To deep throat your partner is a quick technique to get lots of salivae to flow. That is why it functions:

- It will trigger your gag reaction when his penis touches the back of your throat. Your body is prompted to generate a lot of salivae quickly. So if you and your partner prefer deep-throat sex, this is the best way to give your boyfriend a sloppy, wet blowout.

Hint

The glans of your man's penis, mainly the underside, are by far the most sensitive area of his penis, as I have explained. Therefore, concentrating your attention on the tip of his penis will be effective in making him tense up and become pleasurably uncomfortable.

The tip of his penis can be enjoyed using various methods.

- **Kissing**: An excellent way to begin your blow job and lengthen it is to kiss the tip of his penis.
- Ideal if you enjoy hearing and watching your boyfriend writhe in exquisite agony. Just recall how you regularly kiss him (on the lips), and you may quickly and easily kiss his penis and balls.
- Give him a few "pecks" while forming a tight lip purse.

- You can gently squeeze the tip of his penis between your lips if you cringe a little and open them.
- Rub your lips over his penis, saliva on them.
- Gently suction his penis with your lips.

The Twister: This extremely delightful and satisfactory blow job technique, which I like to call the Twister, may be performed using your tongue and a lot of salivae. Start moving your tongue slowly in a circular pattern around the top of his penis while steadily holding it in one or both of your hands. However, this excellent bj method alone is sufficient to send him to a booming climax. You can change direction and speed to provide some diversity.

Deep Throat: Deep throating your man is a more sophisticated blow job method, but when done correctly, it can deeply pleasure and sexually satisfy your man. The back of your throat is responsible for this additional enjoyment. He will finally get so deep in your mouth that the tip of his penis will touch your tonsils and the back of your throat.

Your partner will find it more pleasurable and stimulating because of the mild spasming of your throat (caused by your gag reflex) and the stimulation of the shaft of his dick from the rest of your mouth and tongue.

The Tip: Some guys have delicate urethral openings. His cum emerges from the tiny slit there, which is located at the top of his penis. When you give him a blow job, try gently licking it; observe his response. He's one of those people that likes it if he does. Switch to a different tactic if he doesn't.

Slip Inside: This less skilled fellatio method is almost as good at giving him great pleasure and stimulation as deep-throating him. You can add another blow job tool to your inventory by taking him into your mouth and massaging or pressing the tip of his penis against the inside of your cheek and tongue.

Use the Roof

Another method for stimulating him is using the roof of your mouth, which builds on the prior process. You'd be mistaken if you assumed that giving him a blow job wouldn't be of any assistance to you.

When you tilt his penis such that the top of his glans rubs against the ridges on the roof of your mouth, the texture is lovely. This approach should probably be avoided if the size of his penis and your mouth prevent you from changing angles or if it would result in him being scraped with teeth.

Use of your fingers and hands is not purely a blow job method. They are a terrific method to rest your mouth and jaw, so use them! Try softly stroking the top of his penis with a lot of saliva or lubricant while he's groaning inexplicably in pleasure.

The Ups and Down

The majority of guys, 87.6%, to be exact, dream of having a blow job; however, if you don't feel very confident the first few times you do it, I recommend sticking to simple blow job techniques like the Up & Down

Before moving on to more complex methods and strategies for providing your partner oral pleasure, including sucking him, it is a good idea to master this first. This will help you feel comfortable giving your boyfriend a blow job.

You need to put your man's penis in your mouth and form a tight "O" shape with your mouth around it to do the Up & Down. You can put pressure around his penis thanks to the "O" shape.

You will bob your head back and forth as you take his penis in and out of your mouth. In particular, bobbing your head up and down is easy to learn if you focus only on the top inch or two of his penis. Once you feel confident doing this, try taking him further and deeper with each stroke to stimulate more and more of his penis.

The risk of inducing your gag response increases as you take him deeper and deeper into your mouth. Do your best not to worry about this. Men generally don't mind if you briefly gag because it's typical.

Where his head and shaft unite is marked by a ridge on his penis. For your male, when stimulated, this ridge is susceptible. When you form the letter "O," try concentrating with your lips on it.

Focusing on this region of his penis also reduces the likelihood that you may gag by simply putting the first 1–2 inches of his penis into your mouth. It's alright to take a break, take a breath, and relax your throat if you feel like you might start gagging.

Double-Tongue Tricks

Two more blow job methods that require your tongue are what I want to share with you. While the other is a little trickier but incredibly fulfilling for your man, the first is simple to do.

1. Soft Sandpaper - Don't let the name deceive you. Your boyfriend will feel great; it

won't feel like sandpaper. I've given it the name "Soft Sandpaper" since you'll be "polishing" your man's penis with your tastebuds in a manner akin to how you would with sandpaper. There, though, the parallels cease.

Start with firmly grasping the penis shaft of your man. Then, stick out your tongue while making it as wet as possible.

Next
With your hand, move the head of his penis across your tongue while keeping your head and tongue in position. His penis should, therefore, only move over your language when your hand moves it. It shouldn't move at all when you speak with your tongue.

His penis will be running across your tongue in this scenario.

You can move it in whatever direction you desire, whether in a circle, up and down, back and forth, or any other action.

The head of his penis is "polished" by your tongue in this manner.

2. Sliding Shaft - To use this method, place his penis as far within your mouth as you feel comfortable holding it there. There is no problem with depths of 2, 4, or 6. It is important to ensure that having it there is convenient for you.

You must slide your tongue backwards along his shaft, starting at the underside of his penis as far as you can comfortably go.

Massage the same region of his post by advancing and reversing it again.

Keep his penis in position while you carry out this. Just keep it in place; don't make it shallower or deeper.

When uncut, BJ uses specific techniques

When your man is circumcised or "cut," most of the blow job techniques mentioned above function best. If your man is uncircumcised or "uncut," some instructions still apply without any modifications, while others do. Some BJ techniques, however, will not be effective at all.

There is, however, no cause for concern. You can only employ a few particular methods on men who haven't had their navels cut off. Uncut boys vary because they have more foreskin, also known as prepuce, which covers the glans partially or entirely. The frenulum on the underside of the glans of uncut men is likewise more pronounced.

Pull it back: When a man is erect, his foreskin gets tighter, but the tightness varies, so you'll need to get acclimated to his foreskin when blowing him. There isn't much room because some foreskin is quite tight when the male is hard.

However, do not draw the foreskin too far back. That may sound strange, but some guys find it uncomfortable to pull the foreskin around. To expose at least a portion of the skull, you do not need to push it as far back as it will go. Foreskin needs to be pulled back to have direct access to the penis head because a man won't feel much stimulation.

Change it up: Pulling back the foreskin allows you to concentrate on the tip of his penis while employing the techniques described above, but this might be overwhelming for an uncut guy. Even though women may not detect a change in sensitivity, a study shows that cut guys are less likely to request that their partner be more gentle on their penis. Instead, they want greater stimulation. You may want to occasionally allow the foreskin to slip back into place because, as you may recall, an uncut guy's glans are more sensitive due to the foreskin.

Use the foreskin: Many uncut men enjoy the satisfying sensation of stroking the foreskin across their glans. Additionally, this is an excellent opportunity to rest your mouth! Additionally, it helps to keep your blow job going for longer by providing him with less stimulation.

Swirl your tongue - When you're ready to re-insert his penis into your mouth, maintain the foreskin over it and slide your tongue between the head of his cock and the foreskin. Make two or three swirls in it. He will enjoy it! While removing the foreskin from his glans, move your tongue around.

Suck and squeeze softly. If a person is uncut, you can orally stimulate his foreskin in

Ask him, but the fun method is to try both and decide for yourself which he prefers: you maintain your finger in his ass throughout orgasm or gently pull it out.

Lube and nails - Lastly, be careful to file or trim your nails before penetrating him anally to prevent cutting yourself or hurting him. Due to the anus' lack of natural lubrication compared to the vagina, lube is also necessary for anal penetration.

three-step trick
The Triple Trick technique, which I use for blow jobs, is my most potent.
The act itself isn't tough, but it does take some coordination. Here's how to go about it:Take your man's penis head in your

mouth and begin doing the Twister on it in part 1. (I cover this technique above).

Part 2 - Begin to jerk him off while performing the Twister simultaneously as you take one hand and wrap it around his shaft.

Thirdly, begin massaging his prostate with a finger that has been greased.

You'll be using all three blow job styles at once, which, as I indicated before, calls for a high level of synchronization.

Giving your man triple the pleasure is as simple as that.
Placing On A Show While Having Fun

simplest definition of Awesome Sauce is just putting something in your mouth, like maple syrup, chocolate syrup, cream, champagne, ice cream, or even ice cubes, as you do your daily blow job.

Suggestions on how to use of them each

- These delectable treats—maple syrup, chocolate syrup, and cream—work well since they are delicious and give your husband a novel yet incredibly pleasurable experience as you fellate him. Just watch out that the warm chocolate syrup you use doesn't burn him if it's warm.

- Ice cubes or ice cream - Although cold sensations are not the most common

Awesome Sauce during oral sex; they are effective at changing things up and keeping your partner on his toes.

- Champagne: There is something quite seductive about it, especially when consumed during a BJ. Consider changing into intimate apparel and cracking open a bottle of champagne the next time you and your man have some alone time. After taking a small taste, start performing fellatio on your man while holding the champagne on your lips.

- But it's not simply the sensations the bubbles give your boyfriend; there's more. Giving your partner a champagne blow job and making him

Reference

1:https://www.womenshealthmag.com/sex-and-love/a28591194/how-to-give-a-good-blow-job/

2:https://www.cosmopolitan.com/sex-love/news/a53969/16-things-i-wish-i-knew-before-i-gave-a-blow-job/

3:https://www.masterclass.com/articles/how-to-give-a-blow-job

4:https://badgirlsbible.com/blowjob-tips

5:https://www.advocate.com/sexy-beast/2018/7/10/24-tips-giving-amazing-head#media-gallery-media-1

Printed in Great Britain
by Amazon